This book has been dedicated to K.A.R.

First published 1993 by
Gorilla Books,
4 Cupar Road, Battersea,
London SW11 4JW

©Gorilla Books 1993

ISBN 1-874419-30-2

68* OF THE BEST GOLF JOKES!

*AVERAGE CONTENTS

ILLUSTRATED!

THE OFFICIAL GOLFING JOKE BOOK

by BEVERLEY BENSON and GRAY JOLLIFFE

A golfer was playing with a pro at St. Andrews. Every hole was a disaster with the ball flying off in all directions.

"I just don't understand it" he says to the pro "what am I doing wrong?"

"You've got shit on the end of your club" replied the pro.

The golfer examines the end of his club closely, "I can't see any shit" he says. The pro says "Not that end, stupid, the other end".

A man takes his dog with him to play golf. He takes a beautiful shot off the first tee and the dog gets up on his hind legs and claps. His second shot was equally good and the dog clapped again. "That's an amazing dog you have there" says his partner, "but what does he do if you hit a bad shot?"

"He does cartwheels" answered the dog's owner.

"How many?" enquired his partner.

"Depends how hard I kick him" comes the reply.

Recently widowed, Mrs Goldberg wanders on to the 18th hole carrying a roll of paper containing her husbands ashes.

"Joseph" she says to the ashes, "all your life you told me that your idea of heaven would be a blow job after a round of golf. "Well" she says taking a deep breath and blowing the ashes away "now you've got it".

A party of four were returning from a golf trip to South Africa when their plane crashed in the jungle.

On regaining consciousness the only surviving member of the group could hear the distant sound of drums. For three days he stumbled through the dense undergrowth - the drum beats getting louder and louder - until he eventually breaks into a clearing.

Sitting in the middle was a big black chieftain banging on the drums with a Ping 3 wood and a driver.

"I must have travelled over 50 miles following the sound of your drums" says the survivor.

"Yes" replies the chieftain, "I'm really getting some distance from these new woods."

One Sunday, a four ball was waiting for the fourth player to arrive.

Twenty minutes late he runs into the changing room. "Sorry chaps, but it is Sunday and I had to toss a coin to decide whether to come and play golf or to take my family to church."

"What took you so long?" they enquired.

"I had to toss it 15 times!"

A golf pro is sitting in a bar in Las Vegas when he sees the most beautiful blonde. He goes over and offers to buy her a drink and they start chatting.

By the end of the evening he is completely besotted and asks the girl to marry him. She agrees and they rush into a wedding palace and get spliced.

Back at the hotel room he tells his new wife "I'm a golf professional, so we will have a wonderful life travelling around the world."

"That sounds fantastic darling" she replies and continues to give him the best blow job he has ever had in his life.

"That was sensational" says the new bridegroom, "by the way what do you do?"

"I'm a hooker" she says.

"Don't worry darling, next time just turn your hand over a little."

My wife made the perfect shot— kept her head down just like I told her.
Sounds like a blow job
Yeah, except perfect shots happen more often

A man was playing with three friends when suddenly he stops, takes off his cap and stands still for a couple of minutes as a funeral cortege passes by in the road.

"That shows a great deal of respect for the dead" remarks one of his pals.

"Naturally" he says, "after all we were married for twenty five years."

There was a three ball waiting to tee off when a man comes up to them and asks if he can join them.

They agree and he plays a terrific round of golf.

Afterwards, in the bar, they invite him to join them the next day.

"I'd love to, but what time do you start?"

"About 9.30am" came the reply.

"I'll be there" says the chap, "but if I'm a few minutes late please wait."

The next morning he arrives on the dot and plays another terrific round, but this time left handed.

Back in the bar, the other three say to him "You're a fantastic player - equally good with your left or right hand. How do you choose which one to play?"

"Simple" he replies, "if my wife is lying on her right side when I wake up I play right handed - if she's on her left I play left handed."

"What happens if she's on her back?"

"Well, thats when I'm a few minutes late!"

A man was shipwrecked on a desert island when, after 15 years, a beautiful blonde in a wet suit emerges from the sea.

"I've been sent to rescue you" she says "but before we leave I must help make up for all your deprivations over the past years. How long is it since you had a smoke?"

"15 years" he replied, so the girl unzips a pocket on her wetsuit and gives him a packet of cigarettes and a lighter.

"How long since your last whisky?"

"15 years." She unzips her pocket and hands him a bottle of Johnny Walker.

"Now" said the girl unzipping the front of her wetsuit "how long since you've played around?"

"Don't tell me you've brought my clubs as well...?"

God and Jesus decide to play golf one day. At the first hole, Jesus hits the ball down the fairway about 280 yards.

When it came to God's turn, he slices the ball badly off to the right but, before it can land, he snaps his fingers and an eagle swoops out of the trees, catches the ball in its beak and starts flying towards the green. God snaps his fingers again and a bolt of lightning flashes down and strikes the eagle who drops the ball which bounces onto the green and straight into the hole.

"Now look dad" says Jesus "what are we doing? Playing golf or just fucking around?"

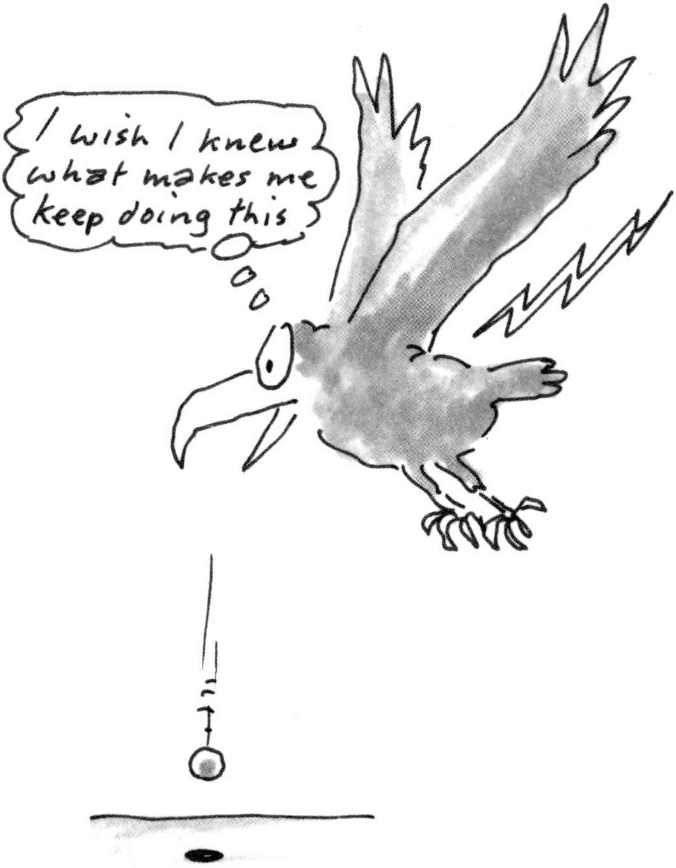
I wish I knew what makes me keep doing this

A nurse comes up to a man in golfing clothes who has been pacing anxiously up and down outside the operating theatre whilst the surgeons were trying to remove a golf ball driven down a player's throat.

"Don't worry" says the nurse "it won't be long now. Are you a relative?"

"No, no lassie. It's my ball."

Two chaps were walking from the club house to the first tee.

"What's up mate?" says one to the other. "You look really fed up."

"It's just that I can't stand the new pro - he just came up behind me and tried to correct my stance."

"Don't be hard on him" says his friend, "he's only trying to improve your game."

"Yes but I was having a pee at the time."

Michael had just been accepted as a member at the local golf club, so wanting to show off, he took his mother-in-law to watch him play a round.

At the first tee, he said to his opponent, "I want to do a really long drive. That's my wife's mother standing over there."

"Don't be silly" said the other, "you'll never be able to hit her at 200 yards."

A golfer was about to hit his ball when the club secretary looks out of the window. "Excuse me" he says "but here at St. Andrews we tee off *between* the markers."

The chap ignores the remark and prepares to swing. "Excuse me," repeats the secretary, "but here we tee off *between* the markers."

The man doesn't even look up and takes up his position once again.

"EXCUSE ME" shouts the secretary. "This is *ROYAL* St. Andrews and we do not tee off in front of the markers".

The golfer sighs, turns to the window, and says "Look mate this is my second shot, OK."

This golfer goes to see his doctor.

"I've got a real problem" he explains "I've become a kleptomaniac and, if I can't get cured, I'm bound to get thrown out of the golf club. Why, I nicked a Pringle sweater from the pro shop last week and then yesterday I stole a putter. Doctor is there anything you can give me?"

"You can try these pills" says the doctor "but if they don't work can you get me a Graphite Driver?"

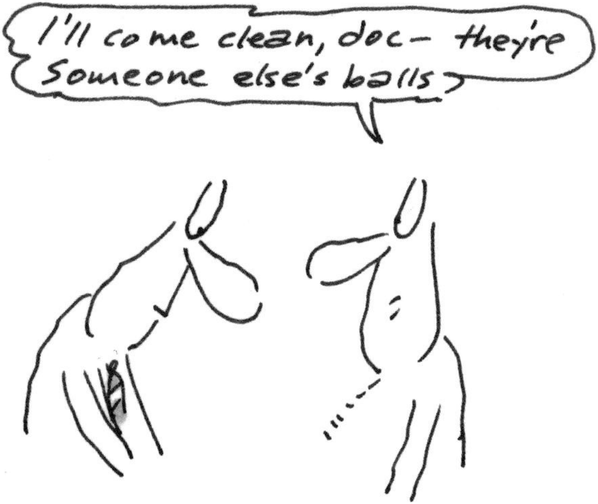
I'll come clean, doc– theyre Someone else's balls

The local Rabbi takes a Saturday off to play golf instead of attending the Synagogue.

He plays like a dream and even gets two holes in one.

Looking up to heaven he says "My life, I've done a terrible thing. I have abandoned my flock to play golf, yet you have given me two holes in one."

A voice from heaven replies, "Sure, but who are you going to tell?"

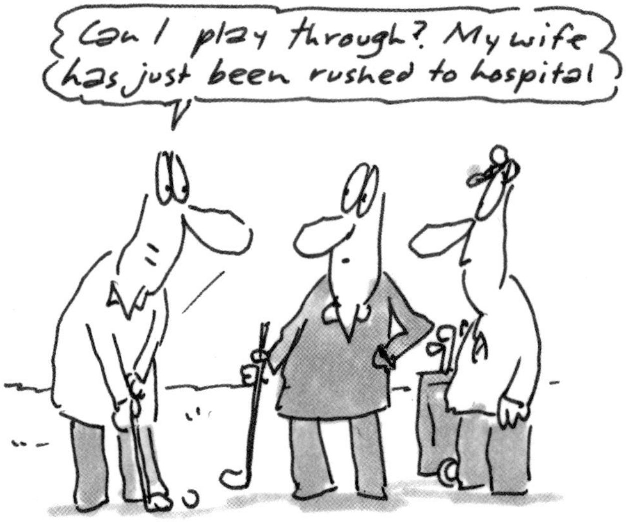
Can I play through? My wife has just been rushed to hospital

An Irishman is walking across the golf course when he gets hit on the head by a golf ball.

He is standing dazed when a golfer rushes out of the bushes.

"Good God man, why didn't you get out of the way", he says sharply.

"And why should I?" replied the Irishman angrily.

"Well I called 'fore'" said the golfer, "and any fool knows that you get out of the way when someone shouts 'fore'."

"Oh really" says the paddy, "fore then" and punches the golfer in the throat.

The golf professional is standing behind a lady golfer trying to help her with her grip.

"Now, hold it firmly but gently. Just a bit more to the right. No, *gently*, don't grip so tightly. Imagine it is your husband's penis.

Well that's a *lot* better, but just take the end out of your mouth."

A couple of guys are playing a round when one has a massive heart attack and dies. Some time later, the partner joins some of his friends in the clubhouse.

"Sorry to hear about Jones," they say. "It must have been horrific for you."

"Tell me about it," he replies. "Play a shot, drag him along. Play a shot, drag him along. I'm exhausted."

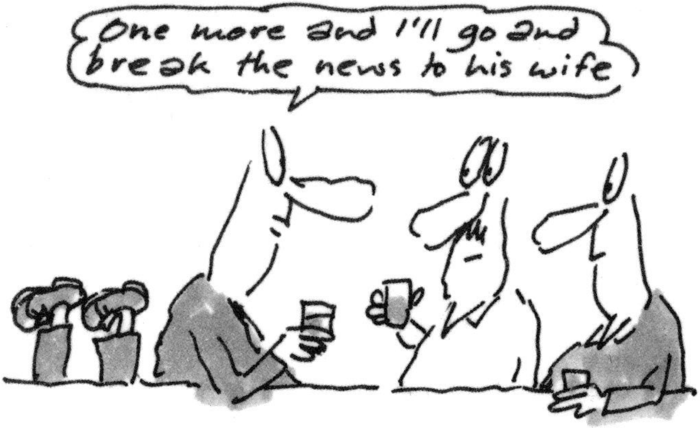
One more and I'll go and break the news to his wife

An environmentalist is playing a round of golf when he slices the ball into a field of buttercups.

"I cannot destroy these lovely flowers," he thinks to himself, so he takes a drop and penalises himself a stroke.

Just as he is about to play, a lady dressed in green appears from behind the bushes.

"That was a wonderful thing you did, saving those buttercups. I am Mother Nature and, as your reward, I am going to grant you as much free butter as you want for the rest of your life."

"Great," responded the golfer, "but where were you when I got caught under the pussy willow."

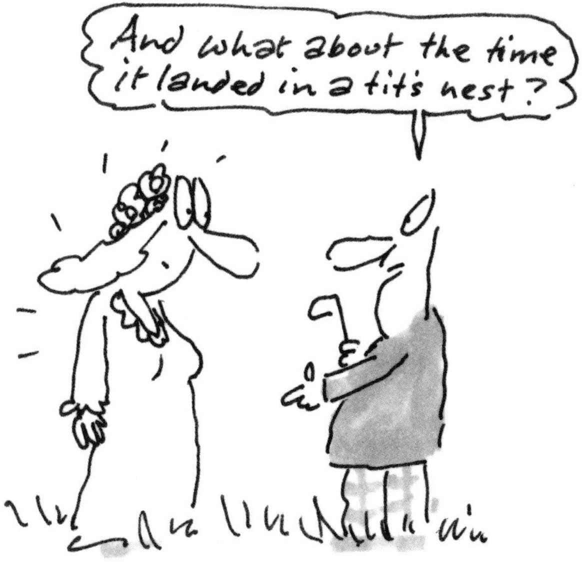
And what about the time it landed in a tit's nest?

Announcing the winners of the club competition, the captain says, "Third prize of a dozen golf balls, to Fred Smith."

"Second prize - a delicious fruit cake, to Brian Hill."

A disgruntled Brian Hill goes up to collect his prize. "How come Fred Smith gets a dozen golf balls for coming third and I get a fruit cake?"

"Ah, but it's a special fruit cake baked by the secretarys wife" explains the captain.

"Screw the secretary's wife" replies Brian.

"No that's the first prize" says the captain.

A chap spends the night with a hooker whilst on a business trip to Japan.

"Oooh, ossi kawa, ossi kawa." she keeps repeating during his performance.

"God, she's really enjoying this" he thinks.

The next day he is playing a round of golf with an important Japanese client. At the 5th hole the client sinks a beautiful putt.

Remembering the night before and the hookers cries of pleasure, he claps his hands and says to his client, "Oooh ossi kawa, ossi kawa."

"What do you mean ouch the wrong hole?" scowls the client.

A couple of chaps playing golf when one slices the ball straight into the woods.

"Play on" he says to his opponent, "I'll just go and find my ball."

30 minutes later, he had not reappeared so his friend goes into the woods looking for him and finds him in a clearing screwing a beautiful blonde.

"What the hell's going on? I thought we were supposed to be playing golf!" he shouts at his friend.

"Well, when I got into the woods I found that my ball had hit this girl on the head and she was lying unconscious."

"That's disgraceful" said his friend "couldn't you just have given her the kiss of life?"

"I did" he replies, "thats how it all started."

I had a terrible day Never made it out of the bunker
Nor did Hitler and he shot himself

Poor Fred just stood on a rake
The only two decent balls he's hit all day

A guy goes up to the bunker and finds a beautiful girl buried up to her neck in sand.

"Help me, please" she pleaded "my husband caught me with another man and has buried me here as a punishment."

"Well" replies the golfer eyeing her voluptuous lips" if I do help you what's in it for me?"

"Would you believe sand!" she replies.

Two clubmen admiring their friend's new Rolls Royce. "It's got everything" he explains proudly, "bar, T.V, stereo, fax, phone."

A passing lady sees a golf tee lying on the drivers seat.

"What's that for?" she enquires.

"Oh that's just for putting your balls on when you are driving" says one of the men. "Goodness" she says "they think of everything at Rolls Royce don't they"

This ageing millionairess was delighted when the new young golf pro dramatically improved her game. "Young man" she bellowed "I insist on buying you something to show my thanks..... anything at all!"

"Well, if you insist" the pro replied "you can buy me some golf clubs."

The next week he received a telegram, "Have bought you Wentworth, and Sunningdale but Gleneagles refused to sell!"

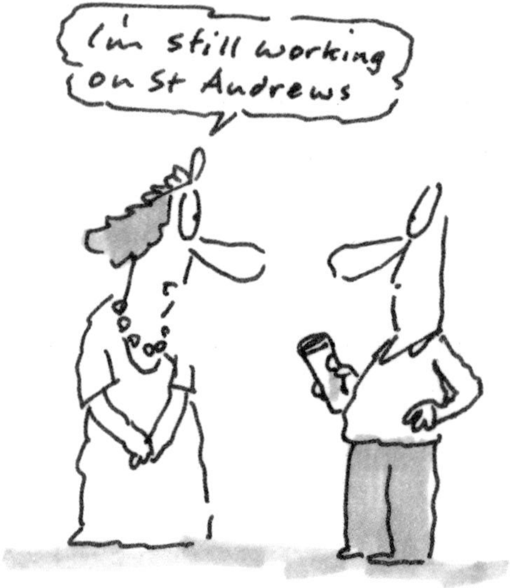
I'm still working on St Andrews

Two golfing friends meet for a drink in the clubhouse bar. "I'll have a scotch and soda," says one hoarsley.

"What happened to your voice?" says the other.

"Bad throat," rasps the first, "Golfing accident."

"What happened?" enquired his friend.

"I was playing a round with Lady Wattisham yesterday. She's a good player but she sliced the ball at the eighth, straight into a field of cows. I went to help her find it but we looked everywhere and there was no sign. We were just about to give up when I had a flash of inspiration. Lifting the tail of the nearest cow, there was the ball lodged firmly in the cow's arse."

"Does this look like yours?," I asked her
Ladyship, and that's when she
wrapped her 9 iron around my neck!"

A couple get knocked over and are killed instantly. When they arrive at the pearly gates they are met by St Peter who offers to show them round. He takes them to a beautiful house "This is where you will live - all your washing, ironing, cooking and other chores will be done for you" he explains. "Over there," he says pointing out of the window, "you will find replicas of four championship golf courses modelled on Augusta, Pebble Beach, Gleneagles and St Andrews. You can play on them as often as you want."

Just then a stunning blonde walks past. "Who is that?" drools the husband. "One of the angels" says St Peter, "they are here for the married men when their wives have a headache."

The husband turns to his wife and smacks her on the face. "What was that for?" she says. "You stupid old bag" he yells "If it wasn't for you putting me on that low cholesterol diet I could have been here years ago."

A golf fanatic who was always trying to improve his game managed to hire Jack Nicklaus's caddy for a round.

At the first tee he enquired "What did Jack use here?" "A 2 iron" replied the caddy, so the golfer hit off with his 2 iron and the ball flew yards down the middle, landing just in front of a big lake situated in front of the green. "What did Jack use here?" enquired the golfer again.

"Oh, he chose the 9 iron" informed the caddy. Taking his 9 iron the golfer swung and hit the ball right into the lake. "I thought you said Jack used a 9 iron here" he said irately. "Yes he did," replied the caddy, "and he put it in the lake as well."

A group of golf enthusiasts go to Le Touquet for the weekend. After a couple of rounds on the Saturday, they decide to partake of the delights of the local brothel. Selecting their partners, they all disappear into their respective bedrooms until, after about 10 minutes, one of the girls comes out onto the landing and says "Madame, qu'est-ce que c'est Mulligan?!"

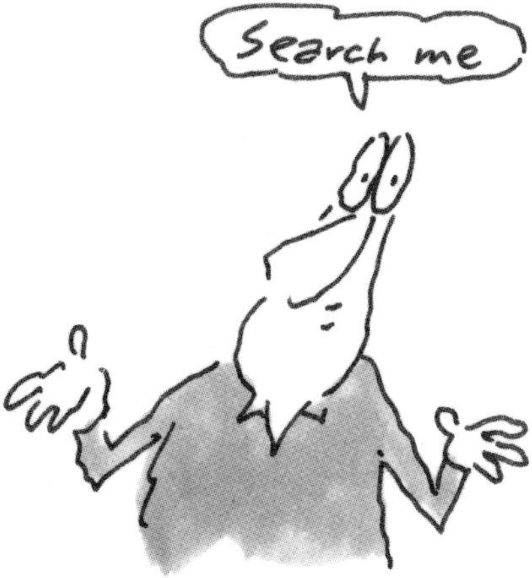
Search me

A chap playing golf with his caddy has a terrible round. Every hole he was four or more shots over par and he was in despair. Eventually they reach the 18th. Standing on the tee he asks the caddy, "What's the par for this hole?" "Par 4 sir, over the water" the caddy replies. "Well if I don't par this time I'm going to throw myself in that water and drown myself". "I don't think so sir," replied the caddy, "you'll never keep your head down long enough."

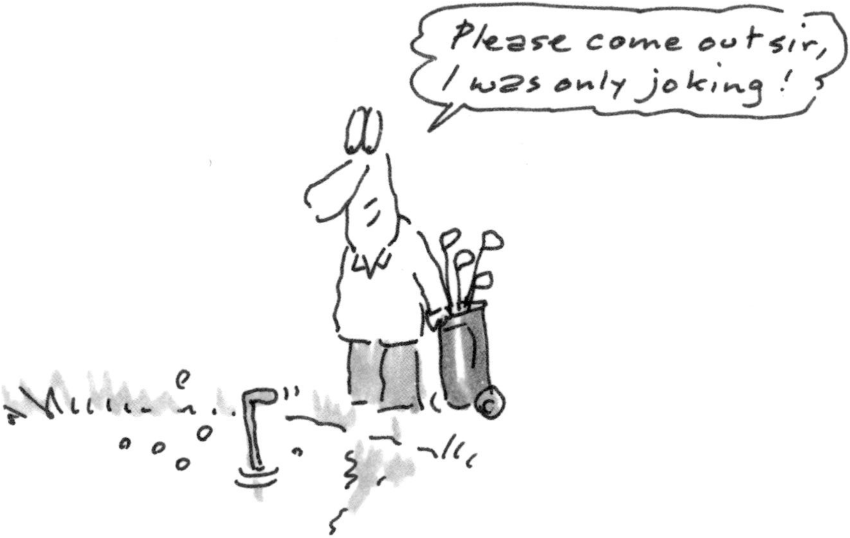
Please come out sir, I was only joking!

Four friends were playing golf where the hazard on the fourth is a deep ravine. Three managed to clear the ravine but the fourth ball dropped down. "I'll play it out" said the golfer and disappears. After a few minutes the ball emerges and the golfer returns.

"How many strokes?" ask the friends.

"Three", he replies.

"How come we heard six?" they ask.

"Three of them were echoes."

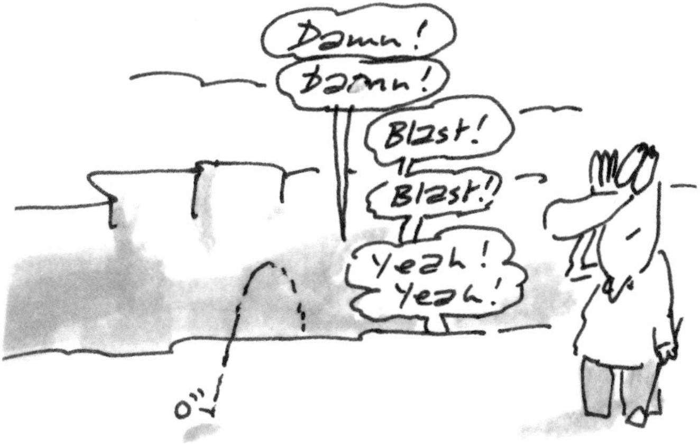
Damn!
Damn!
Blast!
Blast!
Yeah! Yeah!

What's the difference between a
bunker and a blow job?

With a blow job you don't shout "Bite!
Bite!"

A guy says to his wife "I've just won £500.000 in a golf tournament. Pack your bags."

"Wow", she says "winter or summer things?!"

"I don't give a toss. Just pack a bag and piss off."

Two male golfers were following behind a pair of ladies and were getting increasingly irritated by their slow pace. "I'll go and ask if we can play through," said one of the golfers to his friend.

He returns, ashen faced. "I'm afraid I couldn't ask," he explained. "When I got close enough I realised that it was my wife playing a round with my mistress! You go."

His friend walks up towards the women, then swings around and returns. "I say" he said, "it's a small world isn't it!"

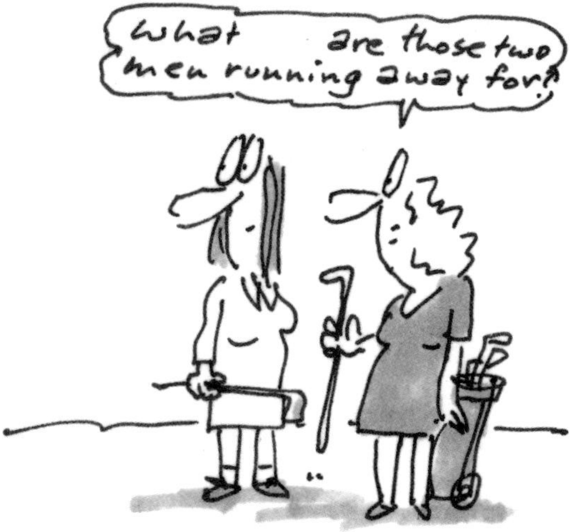
What are those two men running away for?

A couple of golfers were following on behind a single player. On the first tee he hit a magnificent drive, then sliced his second shot into the rough. His third shot cleared the long grass and landed on the green, followed by a fourth that missed the hole and rolled off the side of the green into a bunker. Six landed him 5 inches from the hole which he missed with his seventh, eventually sinking the ball with his eighth.

"I hope you don't mind me saying" said one of the golfers watching this performance, "but your play is very erratic." "Not at all old chap," replied the player, "I'm just practising for the mixed foursomes."

A man is putting on the 7th green when he hears a hiss from behind the bushes. He looks round and a voice says "Have you got any paper, mate?" Irritated, the golfer turns away and starts to putt. "Excuse me, mate, I'm desperate. If you haven't any paper, how about an old golf card?"

The golfer looks away again. Suddenly, a hand appears above the bush waving a £10 note. "For Christ's sake man, at least give me two fivers for a tenner?"

Bill's just murdered his wife – he hit her six times with a five iron!
My God – that's three over par

Coach says I'm always standing too close to the ball
That's not unusual
After I've hit it?

There's these two old club members who have never played together before. They get on the first tee and one tees off, putting his ball about 6 inches in front of the marker. The other member says, "I'm afraid you're in front of the marker."

But he takes no notice, hits the ball off and on the next tee again this man tees off about 8 or 9 inches in front of the marker. So the other says "You're in front of the marker, sir."

Again he takes no notice and this goes on hole after hole after hole - he's constantly in front of the marker. The other player *suddenly* realises the guy is deaf. So he thinks, "Oh, right, if he does it again, I'll give him a real shout." So on the next hole again he's about a foot in front of the marker so he shouts, "Excuse me! You're a foot in front."

The first member says, "You call me
what you like - I'm still 2-up!"

Paddy's working up the golf course, raking the bunkers. A ball bounces onto the green, and plops across into the bunker where he's raking. He picks it up and throws it onto the green and it drops in the hole.

When the player arrives he is so delighted to see that he's got a hole in one that he grabs hold of Paddy, and says, "Come and have a drink on me."

Three whiskies later, Paddy returns to the bunker when another ball sails over the green and drops in front of his rake. Paddy picks it up, and throws it into the hole.

Up comes the player, thrilled, and drags Paddy back to the club house and pours a few pints down him.

Back out in the bunker, staggering across the 18th green another ball

comes over, 2 bounces, straight down
the hole. "Fuck this!" Paddy says and
removes the ball from the hole, "I've
had enough drink for one day!"

Two guys complaining bitterly to the Secretary that they've had the slowest round they've ever had in their lives - they've been stuck 6 hours behind this 4-ball.

The secretary looks out and says, "Ah, yes, well, now those gentlemen have a special concession to play here." They're from the local blind home but they shouldn't have held you up - I'll go and have a word with them."

One guy says, "Oh, please no, we're really terribly embarrassed now. It's amazing to think that four blind guys can still play golf."

"Oh yes" said the Secretary "They've got these little golf balls with individual electronic bleepers in them and they each make a different tone so each man can find his own ball.

The other guy scowls and says "Fuck 'em. With balls like that they could play at night!"

What's that lump in your trousers Mr Pilkins?
Golf balls
Is that as painful as tennis elbow?

I've just got a new set of golf clubs for my wife
So who's the sucker?

A chap about to putt on the 15th when a naked women rushed past. Seconds later a man in a white coat appears in hot pursuit, followed by a second man carrying two buckets of sand.

"What on earth's going on?" says the golfer.

"Oh, she's just escaped from the loony bin," pants the man, "and we've trying to catch her."

"Well, why are you carrying those buckets?" says the golfer. "Oh, they're my handicap. I caught her last time."

A chap is just about to tee off when he puts on a pair of red tinted spectacles.

"I didn't know you wore glasses" said his chum.

"I don't. These are special golfing glasses" he says. "When I look through them, I see one small fairway and one larger fairway. I aim for the large one and it goes straight down the middle. When I putt I see one small hole and one large hole - I aim for the large one and sink the ball."

"They sound fantastic, where can I buy some?" enquires the friend.

"Oh, there is a down side," he replies, "when I go for a pee, I see a big dick and a small dick. I know the big one isn't mine so I put it away and always end up peeing down my trousers."

A golfer playing at a strange club goes into the changing room to have a shower. Naked under the spray he hears ladies voices and realises, to his horror, that he is in the wrong changing room.

Having only one towel, he decides to cover his head and make a run for it. As he dashed by, one lady says to the other, "Did you see that? It's certainly not my husband." "Or mine" replies the second. "He's not even a club member!" says the third.

A guy goes to the golf course, he fancies playing a round of golf on his own. When he gets there, the pro in the club house says, "We've got this new robot caddy that you can go round with. It's great, gives you loads of instructions."

So he plays a fantastic round of golf and the robot is a great help and teaches him a lot.

A month later he goes back and says, "Is that robot caddy I played golf with the other day available?"

The pro says, "No, I'm afraid not, we had to get rid of it."

He says, "Oh, why's that?"

"Well, because when the sun shone it used to reflect off the shiny metal and dazzle all the other players, so we had to get rid of it."

And the guy says, "So why didn't you just paint it black?"

The guy replies "Well in fact we did but it always turned up late and then things started going missing from the Locker Room."

An enthusiastic golfer came home to dinner.

During the meal his wife said "Willie tells me he caddied for you this afternoon."

"Well what do you know" said Willie's father, "I thought I'd seen that boy before."

"I would move heaven and earth to be able to break 100 on this course" sighed the golfer.

"I'd concentrate on the heaven" replied his weary caddy, "you've already moved most of the earth!"

One hooker talking to another after a golf competition in Augusta. "I got £5000 from one chap" boasts one of the hookers. "Whatever for?" enquired her friend. "Well, I had to take off my clothes and let him beat me with a 5 iron", she replied. "How long for?" asks the friend. "Oh, until I gave the £5000 back," came the reply!

A novice joins a golf club and, on his very first round, gives the ball an almighty swipe and gets a hole in one.

At the second tee he swipes again - the ball lands on the green, rolls towards the hole and just plops in. The novice turns to his partner, white and trembling. "What's the problem?" asks the partner. "Christ, I thought I'd missed that one" replies the novice.

An old man is playing the final putt on the 18th green when he spies a snail. He goes over to it and, taking his driver, he whacks it into the distance. "What on earth did you do that for?" asks his partner.

"That bastard's been following me around all week" responded the old man.

A golfer arrives in Heaven and Saint Peter takes him on the grand tour, including the celestial golf course. When they reach the 3rd hole they come across a man whose ball has landed in a ditch 300 yards from the green. The man looks at his caddy and says "I think I can make it with a 7 iron."

The watching golfer turns to Saint Peter in amazement, "Who the hell does he think he is?" he enquires, "Jesus?"

"No, it is Jesus" replied Saint Peter, "but he thinks he's Arnold Palmer."

This women wants to learn to play golf. The pro takes her out onto the practice ground. "Right" he says, "let's see you hold the club."

She takes the club in both hands and the pro says, "Perfect, I thought you hadn't played before?"

"Right, now address the ball", says the pro and the women stands up to the ball perfectly. "You sure you've never played before?" asks the pro.

The pro continues, "OK, now hit it." The women, with arms outstretched in front of her, raises the club and brings it back down on top of the ball!

This novice player tees off the 18th, and hits a massive slice over the trees; he puts another ball down and tees off again. He and his partner finish the game.

As they come off the 18th, the Captain comes up to them and asks if either of them hit a ball over the trees. The novice admits it was him.

The Captain explains that the ball hit a motorcyclist on the motorway and killed him stone dead.

"Oh no!" groans the novice.

"The motorcyclist," continues the Captain "crashed into a mini carrying four nuns who swerved into the path of a coach killing them outright."

"Oh my god!" mumbles the novice.

"The coach, carrying a party of 40 schoolchildren skidded across the central reservation and down the embankment into the path of an oncoming 125 - the children are all dead and there are three derailed carriages..."

"Stop!" exclaimed the novice, "isn't there anything I can do!!!"

The Captain ponders for a second, puts his hands together as if gripping a club and calmly replies, "Well, you could try holding your right over a little more!!"

A guy goes to the doctor complaining of being tired all day. "Describe your routine" says the doctor.

"Well, I awake at 6.00am, make love to my wife then have breakfast. I make love to her again then play 18 holes of golf. After nipping home at lunchtime to give her one, I play another 18 holes then go home and make love. Most evenings I go to the driving range for a couple of hours, go home and make love to my wife - have a late supper, make love, go to bed and make love."

"Well", says the doctor "I think that you are making love too often."

"Oh," replies the man "you don't think it's the wanking at the golf club then?"

Two chaps are playing the 7th at Wentworth when a girl does a massive slice off the tee on the 8th, hitting one of the chaps on the 7th. He's doubled up in pain, his hands clutching his groin.

She goes up to him. "I'm a nurse, may I help?"

Gratefully, the chap accepts.

She unzips his flies and gently and expertly massages the injured part for quite some time.

Finally, she asks, "Now then, is that better?"

Nodding, the chap replies, "Yeah, but I still think you've broken my thumb!!"

A golfer at confession tells the priest he has sinned.

"In what way, my son?" enquires the priest.

"I swore on the golf course, Father. I was having a fantastic round then hit the ball into the bunker on the 18th."

"So then you swore my son, I understand."

"No Father, I hit it clean out and it bounced onto the green and landed in a divot."

"Well," says the Father "being a golfing man myself, I can understand that you would be tempted to swear then."

"No Father, I didn't swear. I chipped it out and it landed two feet from the hole."

"Don't tell me," sighed the priest "you missed the fucking putt."

A golfer went round with the pro and had a disastrous round.

"Have you got any suggestions for improving my game?" he asks in despair.

"Try cutting 6 inches off your clubs" says the pro.

"Will that improve my swing?" the golfer enquires.

"No," comes the reply "but they'll fit in the dustbin better."